As Burns Said...

*A Collection of Quotations
from the Writings of
Scotland's Greatest Poet,
Robert Burns*

Compiled by
Arnold O'Hara

Alloway Publishing
AYR

For Mona
with love and thanks

INTRODUCTION

I have compiled this collection of quotations from the prolific pen of Robert Burns for two reasons. Firstly, as an avid collector of extracts from the writings of Burns over many years I felt compelled to organise them in some sort of order. Secondly, for a long time I have been searching for a book such as this without success.

Burns, because of the wide variety of subjects he dealt with in his works, has provided us with so much that is applicable to so many different aspects of life. It is a tribute to the poet's remarkable powers of perception and his keen observation of the human condition that many of the words which he wrote are as relevant today as they were in the eighteenth century.

Robert Burns himself was an enthusiastic collector of quotations and many of these can be found in his correspondence. In 1792 he told Mrs Frances Dunlop, an admirer of his, in a letter, "I pick up my favourite quotations, and store them in my mind as ready armour, offensive or defensive, amid the struggle of this turbulent existence".

I hope this book will appeal not only to students of the works of Robert Burns but also to those who are looking for appropriate quotations for speeches, essays and articles on more general matters. I have arranged the quotations under the headings of subjects and listed the subjects in alphabetical order for the convenience of the reader. Like anyone else undertaking such a task I have had to be selective, but many of the quotations contained here are among my personal favourites.

Arnold O'Hara

© ARNOLD O'HARA

First Published in 1987
by
Alloway Publishing Ltd.,
Ayr.

Reprinted 1989

—

Printed in Scotland
by
Walker & Connell Ltd.,
Hastings Square, Darvel,
Ayrshire.

—

ISBN 0-907526-30-6

CONDITIONS OF SALE

CONTENTS

CONTENTS (Continued)

A page reference is given with each quotation. This refers to the page where the full text of the poem can be found in Alloway Publishing's Bicentenary Editions of The Complete Works of Robert Burns.

ADVICE

Had I to guid advice but harkit,   listened
I might, by this, hae led a market,
Or strutted in a bank and clarkit   clerked
    My cash account:
While here, half-mad, half-fed, half-sarkit,   half-clothed
        Is a' th' amount.
            The Vision   (p. 114)

In ploughman phrase, 'God send you speed,'
    Still daily to grow wiser;
And may ye better reck the rede,   heed; advice
    Than ever did th' adviser!
        Epistle To A Young Friend   (p. 221)

    O Tam, had'st thou but been sae wise,
As taen thy ain wife Kate's advice!   to have taken
She tauld thee weel thou was a skellum,   good-for-nothing
A blethering, blustering, drunken blellum;   chattering; babbler
        Tam O Shanter   (p. 410)

    Ah, gentle dames, it gars me greet,   makes; weep
To think how monie counsels sweet,   many
How monie lengthen'd sage advices
The husband frae the wife despises!
        Tam O Shanter   (p. 410)

To sum up all: be merry, I advise;
And as we're merry, may we still be wise!
            Address spoken by
            Miss Fontenelle   (p. 508)

AYR

    This truth fand honest Tam o Shanter,   found
As he frae Ayr ae night did canter;   one
(Auld Ayr, whom ne'er a town surpasses,
For honest men and bonie lasses).
        Tam O Shanter   (p. 410)

But round my heart the ties are bound,
The heart transpierc'd with many a wound;
These bleed afresh, those ties I tear,
To leave the bonie banks of Ayr.

> *The Gloomy Night*
> *Is Gath'ring Fast   (p. 250)*

Farewell my friends! farewell my foes!
My peace with these, my love with those --
The bursting tears my heart declare,
Farewell, my bonie banks of Ayr!

> *The Gloomy Night*
> *Is Gath'ring Fast   (p. 250)*

That sacred hour can I forget?
    Can I forget the hallow'd grove,
Where, by the winding Ayr, we met,
    To live one day of parting love?

> *Thou Lingering Star   (p. 372)*

O Ayr! my dear, my native ground,
Within thy presbyterial bound
A candid lib'ral band is found
        Of public teachers,
As men, as Christians too, renown'd,
        An manly preachers.

> *Epistle To The*
> *Rev. John McMath   (p. 129)*

    'Twas in that season, when a simple Bard,
Unknown and poor -- simplicity's reward! --
Ae night, within the ancient brugh of Ayr,   One; burgh
By whim inspir'd, or haply prest wi care,
He left his bed, and took his wayward route,

> *The Brigs Of Ayr   (p. 244)*

Lord, hear my earnest cry and pray'r,
Against that Presbyt'ry o Ayr!
Thy strong right hand, Lord, mak it bare
        Upo' their heads!
Lord, visit them, an dinna spare,   do not
        For their misdeeds!

> *Holy Willie's Prayer   (p. 93)*

But Beauty, how frail and how fleeting!
    The bloom of a fine summer's day!

        Adown Winding Nith   (p. 497)

There's ane they ca' Jean, I'll warrant ye've seen   one
    As bonie a lass or as braw, man;   well set up
But for sense and guid taste she'll vie wi the best,
    And a conduct that beautifies a', man.

        The Ronalds Of
        The Bennals (p. 76)

Sweetly deckt with pearly dew
    The morning rose may blow;
But cold successive noontide blasts
    May lay its beauties low.

        On The Death Of
        John McLeod, Esq.   (p. 283)

Awa wi your witchcraft o Beauty's alarms,
The slender bit beauty you grasp in your arms!
O, gie me the lass that has acres o charms!   give
O, gie me the lass wi the weel-stockit farms!

      A Lass Wi A Tocher   (p. 563)   Dowry

Your Beauty's a flower in the morning that blows,
And withers the faster the faster it grows;

      A Lass Wi A Tocher   (p. 563)

An e'en when this Beauty your bosom has blest,
The brightest o Beauty may cloy when possess'd;

      A Lass Wi A Tocher (p. 563)

Wit and Grace and Love and Beauty
    In ae constellation shine!   one
To adore thee is my duty,
    Goddess o this soul o mine.

      Bonie Wee Thing   (p. 446)

For a' that, an a' that,
    It's comin yet for a' that,
That man to man, the world o'er
    Shall brithers be for a' that.

        A Man's A Man For A' That   *(p. 535)*

Like brethren in a common cause,
    We'd on each other smile, man,
And equal rights and equal laws
    Wad gladden every isle, man.

        The Tree Of Liberty   *(p. 478)*

O thou, my elder brother in misfortune,
By far my elder brother in the Muse,
With tears I pity thy unhappy fate!
Why is the Bard unfitted for the world,
Yet has so keen a relish of its pleasures?

        Apostrophe To Fergusson   *(p. 269)*

Not but I hae a richer share
      Than monie ithers;   many
But why should ae man better fare,   one
      And a' men brithers?

        Epistle To Dr. Blacklock   *(p. 370)*

And at his elbow, Souter Johnie,   Cobbler
His ancient, trusty, drouthy cronie: thirsty companion
Tam lo'ed him like a very brither;
They had been fou for weeks thegither.   drunk; together

        Tam O Shanter   *(p. 410)*

Then gently scan your brother man,
    Still gentler sister woman;
Tho they may gang a kennin wrang,   go a little wrong
    To step aside is human:

        Address To
        The Unco Guid   *(p. 74)*   Rigidly Righteous

Ev'n winter bleak has charms to me,
When winds rave thro the naked tree;
Or frosts on hills of Ochiltree
   Are hoary gray;
Or blinding drifts wild-furious flee,   fly
   Dark'ning the day!

    Epistle To William Simpson *(p. 107)*

Why am I loth to leave this earthly scene?
  Have I so found it full of pleasing charms?
Some drops of joy with draughts of ill between;
  Some gleams of sunshine 'mid renewing storms?

    Stanzas, On The Same Occasion *(p. 54)*

O, could the Fates but name the price
  Would bless me with your charms and you,
With frantic joy I'd pay it thrice,
  If human art and power could do!

    Sylvander To Clarinda *(p. 301)*

The charms o the min', the langer they shine mind
  The mair admiration they draw, man;   more
While peaches and cherries, and roses and lilies,
  They fade and they wither awa, man.

    The Ronalds Of The Bennals *(p. 76)*

Her lips, more than the cherries bright —
  A richer dye has graced them
They charm the admiring gazer's sight,
  And sweetly tempt to taste them.

    Young Peggy *(p. 125)*

The tender thrill, the pitying tear,
The generous purpose, nobly dear,
The gentle look that rage disarms —
These are all immortal charms.

    My Peggy's Charms *(p. 297)*

I mourn thro the gay, gaudy day,
        As hopeless I muse on thy charms;
But welcome the dream o sweet slumber!
        For then I am lockt in thine arms, Jessie —
            For them I am lockt in thine arms!

*Here's A Health To
Ane I Loe Dear   (p. 565)*   One; Love

Low in your wintry beds, ye flowers,
        Again ye'll flourish fresh and fair;
Ye birdies, dumb in with'ring bowers,
        Again ye'll charm the vocal air;

The Braes O Ballochmyle   (p. 126)

O, sweet grows the lime and the orange,
        And the apple on the pine;
But a' the charms o the Indies
        Can never equal thine.

*Will Ye Go To
The Indies My Mary   (p. 468)*

CONTENTMENT

Contented wi little and cantie wi mair,   joyful; more
Whene'er I forgather wi Sorrow and Care,
I gie them a skelp, as they're creepin alang,   smack
Wi a cog o guid swats and an auld Scottish sang cup; ale

*Contented Wi Little
And Cantie Wi Mair   (p. 531)*

Wi weans I'm mair than weel contented   children
Heav'n sent me ane mair than I wanted!

The Inventory   (p. 195)

But how it comes, I never kend yet,   knew
They re maistly wonderfu contented.
An buirdly chiels, an clever hizzies,   stout lads, girls
Are bred in sic a way as this is.   such

The Twa Dogs   (p. 140)

O Scotia! my dear, my native soil!
        For whom my warmest wish to Heaven is sent!
Long may thy hardy sons of rustic toil
        Be blest with health, and peace, and sweet content

The Cotter's Saturday Night   (p. 147)

I'll set me down, and sing and spin,   sit
While laigh descends the summer sun,   low
Blest wi content, and milk and meal —
O, leeze me on my spinnin-wheel.   blessings

        Bessy And Her Spinnin-Wheel   (p. 452)

We may be poor, Robie and I;
    Light is the burden luve lays on;
Content and loove brings peace and joy:
    What mair hae Queens upon a throne?   more; have

        The Country Lass   (p. 455)

CRITICS

    But O thou bitter step-mother and hard,
To thy poor fenceless, naked child — the bard
. . . .
In naked feeling, and in aching pride,
He bears th' unbroken blast from ev'ry side:
Vampyre booksellers drain him to the heart,
And scorpion critics cureless venom dart.

        To Robert Graham, Esq.
        Of Fintry   (p. 431)

How Genius, th' illustrious father of fiction,
Confounds rule and law, reconciles contradiction,
I sing: If these mortals, the critics should bustle,
I care not, not I: let the critics go whistle!

        Inscribed To The Right Hon.
        C.J. Fox   (p. 356)

Nae mair we see his levee door
Philosophers and Poets pour,
And toothy Critics by the score,
      In bloody raw;   row
The adjutant o a' the core,   band
      Willie's awa!

        Lament For The Absence
        Of William Creech, Publisher   (p. 277)

Critics — appall'd, I venture on the name;
Those cut-throat bandits in the paths of fame;
Bloody dissectors, worse than ten Monroes: Alexander Monroe,
He hacks to teach, they mangle to expose.   professor of anatomy

To Robert Graham, Esq.
Of Fintry   (p. 431)

Your critic-folk may cock their nose,
And say, 'How can you e'er propose,
You wha ken hardly verse frae prose,
          To mak a sang!'
But, by your leave, my learned foes,
          Ye're maybe wrang.

Epistle To J. Lapraik   (p. 101)

CRUELTY

Inhuman man! curse on thy barb'rous art,
      And blasted be thy murder-aiming eye;
      May never pity soothe thee with a sigh,
Nor never pleasure glad thy cruel heart!

The Wounded Hare   (p. 354)

Tho cruel fate should bid us part
      Far as the pole and line,
Her dear idea round my heart
      Should tenderly entwine.

Tho Cruel Fate   (p. 251)

I see the children of affliction
Unaided, through thy curs'd restriction.
I've seen the oppressor's cruel smile
Amid his hapless victim's spoil;

Line Written On A Banknote   (p. 223)

Sure Thou, Almighty, canst not act
      ,From cruelty or wrath!
O, free my weary eyes from tears,
      Or close them fast in death!

Prayer Under The Pressure
Of Violent Anguish   (p. 55)

All hail, inexorable lord!
At whose destruction-breathing word,
　　The mightiest empires fall!
Thy cruel, woe-delighted train,
The ministers of grief and pain,
　　A sullen welcome, all!

　　　　　To Ruin　(p. 53)

Thou saw the fields laid bare an waste,
An weary winter comin fast,
An cozie here, beneath the blast,
　　　Thou thought to dwell,
Till crash! the cruel coulter past　　　　ploughshare
　　　Out thro thy cell.

　　　　To A Mouse　(p. 131)

DEATH

O what is death but parting breath?
　　On many a bloody plain
I've dared his face, and in this place
　　I scorn him yet again!

　　　　McPherson's Farewell　(p. 308)

Death, oft I've fear'd thy fatal blow!
　　Now fond I bare my breast;
O, do thou kindly lay me low
　　With him I love, at rest!

　　　　A Mother's Lament　(p. 334)

O Death, had'st thou but spar'd his life,
　　Whom we this day lament!
We freely wad exchanged the wife,
　　And a' been weel content.

　　　　Epigram On Said Occasion　(p. 209)

The tyrant Death, with grim control
　　May seize my fleeting breath,
But tearing Peggy from my soul
　　Must be a stronger death.

　　　　　Where, Braving Angry
　　　　　Winter's Storms　(p. 298)

Is it departing pangs my soul alarms?
     Or death's unlovely, dreary, dark abode?
For guilt, for guilt, my terrors are in arms:
     I tremble to approach an angry God,
And justly smart beneath His sin-avenging rod.

> *Stanzas, On The Same*
> *Occasion   (p. 54)*

'O Death! the poor man's dearest friend,
     The kindest and the best!
Welcome the hour my aged limbs
     Are laid with thee at rest!
The great, the wealthy fear thy blow,
     From pomp and pleasure torn;
But, oh! a blest relief for those
     That weary-laden mourn!'

> *Man Was Made To Mourn —*
> *A Dirge   (p. 123)*

'Tis not the surging billows' roar,
'Tis not that fatal, deadly shore;
Tho death in ev'ry shape appear,
The wretched have no more to fear;

> *The Gloomy Night*
> *Is Gath'ring Fast   (p. 250)*

But O! fell Death's untimely frost,
     That nipt my flower sae early!
Now green's the sod, and cauld's the clay,
     That wraps my Highland Mary!

> *Highland Mary   (p. 470)*

There's Death in the cup, so beware!
     Nay, more — there is danger in touching;
But who can avoid the fell snare?
     The man and his wine's so bewitching!

> *Inscription On A Goblet   (p. 362)*

But lest you think I am uncivil
To plague you with this draunting drivel,　　　tedious
Adjuring a' intentions evil,
　　　I quat my pen:　　　quit
The Lord preserve us frae the Devil!
　　　Amen! Amen!

　　　　Epistle To Colonel
　　　　De Peyster   (p. 564)

How Fortune wrought us good from evil:
Let no man, then, despise the Devil,
As who should say: 'I ne'er can need him,'
Since we to scoundrels owe our Freedom.

　　　　On Glenriddell's Fox
　　　　Breaking His Chain   (p. 426)

Dear ·————, I'll gie ye some advice,
　　　You'll tak it no uncivil:
You shouldna paint at angels, man,
　　　But try to paint the Devil.

To paint an angel's kittle wark,　　　ticklish work
　　　Wi Nick there's little danger;
You'll easy draw a lang-kent face,　　　long-known
　　　But no sae weel a stranger.

　　　　Epigram Addressed
　　　　To An Artist   (p. 270)

'I faught at land, I faught at sea,
　　　At hame I faught my auntie, O;
But I met the Devil an Dundee,
　　　On the braes o Killiecrankie, O.

　　　　Killiecrankie   (p. 398)

'We'll mak our maut, and we'll brew our drink,　　　malt
　　　We'll laugh, sing, and rejoice, man!
And monie braw thanks to the meikle black Deil,　　　fine, great
　　　That danc'd awa wi th' Exciseman.

　　　　The Deil's Awa wi　　　Devil's Away
　　　　Th' Exciseman   (p. 467)　　　With

The Deil he could na skaith thee,   not harm
    Or aught that wad belang thee;
He'd look into thy bonie face,
    And say: — 'I canna wrang thee!'

        Saw Ye Bonie Lesley   (p. 435)

As father Adam first was fool'd,
    A case that's still to common,
Here lies a man a woman ruled —
    The Devil ruled the woman.

           Epitaph On A
           Henpecked Squire   (p. 209)

DRINK

Leeze me on drink! it gies us mair   Blessings
    Than either school or college;
It kindles wit, it waukens lear,   learning
    It pangs us fou o knowledge: crams; full

        The Holy Fair   (p. 133)

See Social Life and Glee sit down,
    All joyous and unthinking
Till, quite transmugrify'd, they're grown
    Debauchery and Drinking:

        Address To   Rigidly
        The Unco Guid   (p. 74)   Righteous

    But to our tale: — Ae market night,
Tam had got planted unco right,   uncommonly
Fast by an ingle, bleezing finely,
Wi reaming swats, that drank divinely: foaming ale

        Tam O Shanter   (p. 410)

    Now, wha this tale o truth shall read,
Ilk man, and mother's son, take heed:
Whene'er to drink you are inclin'd,
Or cutty sarks rin in your mind,
Think! ye may buy the joys o'er dear:
Remember Tam o Shanter's mare.

        Tam O Shanter   (p. 410)

And they hae taen his very heart's blood,   have taken
  And drank it round and round;
And still the more and more they drank,
  Their joy did more abound.

    John Barleycorn:
    A Ballad   (p. 60)

In honest Bacon's ingle-neuk,   fireside corner
  Here maun I sit and think;
Sick o the warld and warld's fock,   folk
  And sick, damn'd sick o drink!

    To William Stewart   (p. 350)

Go fetch to me a pint o wine,
  And fill it in a silver tassie;   goblet
That I may drink before I go,
  A service to my bonie lassie:

    The Silver Tassie   (p. 342)

But first, before you see Heaven's glory,
May ye get monie a merrie story,   many
Monie a laugh, and monie a drink,
And ay eneugh o needfu clink!   always enough;
          coin

    Epistle To James Tennant
    Of Glenconner   (p. 200)

FAME

Great is thy pow'r an great thy fame;
Far kend an noted is thy name;   known
An tho yon lowin heugh's thy hame,   flaming hollow
  Thou travels far;
An faith! thou's neither lag, nor lame,   backward
  Nor blate, nor scaur.   bashful, afraid

    Address To The Deil   (p. 161)

Go, Fame, an canter like a filly
Thro a' the streets an neuks o Killie;   corners; Kilmarnock
Tell ev'ry social honest billie   person
  To cease his grievin;
For, yet unskaith'd by Death's gleg gullie,   unharmed; sharp knife
  Tam Samson's leevin!   living

    Tam Samson's Elegy   (p. 239)

In Poverty's low barren vale,
    Thick mists obscure involv'd me round;
Though oft I turn'd the wistful eye,
    Nae ray of fame was to be found;

> *Lament For James,*
> *Earl of Glencairn   (p. 423)*

Ambition is a meteor-gleam;
Fame a restless idle dream;
Pleasures, insects on the wing
Peace, th' tend'rest flow'r of spring.

> *Verses In Friar's*
> *Carse Hermitage   (p. 324)*

Know thou, O stranger to the fame
Of this much lov'd, much honour'd name!
(For none that knew him need be told)
A warmer heart Death ne'er made cold.

> *Epitaph For*
> *Robert Aitken Esq.   (p. 71)*

'I taught thy manners-painting strains,
The loves, the ways of simple swains,
Till now, o'er all my wide domains
        Thy fame extends;
And some, the pride of Coila's plains,
        Become thy friends.

> *The Vision   (p. 114)*

Heard ye o the tree o France,
    I watna what's the name o't;   don't know
Around it a' the patriots dance,
    Weel Europe kens the fame o't.   knows

> *The Tree Of Liberty   (p. 478)*

Is there nae poet, burning keen for fame,
Will bauldly try to gie us plays at hame?   give
For Comedy abroad he need na toil;
A knave and fool are plants of every soil.

> *Scots Prologue For*
> *Mrs. Sutherland   (p. 399)*

And bless auld Coila large and long,
 With mulitiplying joys;
Lang may she stand to prop the land,
 The flow'r of ancient nations,
And Burnses spring her fame to sing
 To endless generations!

   Nature's Law *(p. 253)*

With awe-struck thought and pitying tears,
 I view that noble, stately dome,
Where Scotia's kings of other years,
 Fam'd heroes! had their royal home:

   Address To Edinburgh *(p. 262)*

FAREWELL

Fareweel to a' our Scottish fame,
 Fareweel our ancient glory!
Fareweel ev'n to the Scottish name,
 Sae famed in martial story!

   Such A Parcel of Rogues
   In A Nation *(p. 460)*

Farewell, old Scotia's bleak domains,
Far dearer than the torrid plains,
 Where rich ananas blow!   pineapples
Farewell, a mother's blessing dear,
A brother's sigh, a sister's tear,
 My Jean's heart-rending throe

   The Farewell *(p. 238)*

Fare-thee-weel, thou first and fairest!
Fare-thee-weel, thou best and dearest!
Thine be ilka joy and treasure,   every
Peace, Enjoyment, Love and Pleasure!

   Ae Fond Kiss *(p. 434)*

When ance life's day draws near the gloamin,   twilight
Then fareweel vacant, careless roamin;
An fareweel cheerful tankards foamin,
       An social noise;
An fareweel dear, deluding Woman,
       The joy of joys!

          Epistle To James Smith   *(p. 169)*

Farewell to the Highlands, farewell to the North,
The birthplace of valour, the country of worth!
Wherever I wander, wherever I rove,
The hills of the Highlands for ever I love.

          My Heart's In The Highlands   *(p. 390)*

Farewell, thou fair day, thou green earth and ye skies,
     Now gay with the broad setting sun!
Farewell, loves and friendships, ye dear tender ties —
     Our race of existence is run!

          The Song Of Death   *(p. 420)*

And fare thee weel, my only luve!
     And fare thee weel, a while!
And I will come again, my luve,
     Tho it were ten thousand mile!

               My Luve Is Like
               A Red, Red Rose   *(p. 517)*

Now a' is done that men can do,
     And a' is done in vain,
My Love and Native Land fareweel,
     For I maun cross the main, my dear —
     For I maun cross the main.

               It Was A' For Our
               Rightfu King   *(p. 594)*

Now farewell light, thou sunshine bright,
     And all beneath the sky!
May coward shame distain his name,
     The wretch that dare not die!

          McPherson's Farewell   *(p. 308)*

Farewell, dear friend! may guid luck hit you,
And 'mong her favourites admit you!
If e'er Detraction shore to smit you,   threaten; smite
      May nane believe him!
And onie Deil that thinks to get you,   any
      Good Lord, deceive him!

    To Mr. John Kennedy   (p. 242)

Then farewell hopes o laurel-boughs,
To garland my poetic brows!
Henceforth I'll rove where busy ploughs
      Are whistling thrang;   at work
An teach the lanely heights and howes   hollows
      My rustic sang.

    Epistle To James Smith   (p. 169)

FATE

    I dread thee, Fate, relentless and severe,
With all a poet's, husband's, father's fear!

    To Robert Fintry, Esq.,
    Of Fintry   (p. 431)

Fate still has blest me with a friend
    In every care and ill;
And oft a more endearing band,
    A tie more tender still.

    Epistle To Davie,
    A Brother Poet   (p. 86)

Such is the fate of simple Bard,
On Life's rough ocean luckless starr'd!
Unskilful he to note the card
      Of prudent lore,
Till billows rage, and gales blow hard,
      And whelm him o'er!

    To A Mountain Daisy   (p. 203)

Ev'n thou who mourn'st the Daisy's fate,
That fate is thine — no distant date;
Stern Ruin's plough-share drives elate,
        Full on thy bloom,
Till crush'd beneath the furrow's weight,
        Shall be thy doom!

        To A Mountain Daisy   *(p. 203)*

'A few seem favourites of Fate,
     In pleasure's lap carest;
Yet think not all the rich and great
     Are likewise truly blest:

         Man Was Made To Mourn
         — A Dirge   *(p. 123)*

Fate gave the word — the arrow sped,
     And pierc'd my darling's heart,
And with him all the joys are fled
     Life can to me impart.

        A Mother's Lament   *(p. 334)*

The star that rules my luckless lot,
Has fated me the russet coat,
And damn'd my fortune to the groat;
        But, in requit,
Has blest me with a random-shot
        O countra wit.   country

        Epistle To James Smith   *(p. 169)*

I'll wander on, wi tentless heed   careless
How never-halting moments speed,
Till Fate shall snap the brittle thread;
        Then, all unknown,
I'll lay me with th' inglorious dead,
        Forgot and gone!

        Epistle To James Smith   *(p. 169)*

The tempest's howl, it soothes my soul,
    My griefs it seems to join;
The leafless trees my fancy please,
    Their fate resemble mine!

> *Winter: A Dirge*   *(p. 50)*

O why should Fate sic pleasures have,   such
    Life's dearest bands untwining?
Or why sae sweet a flower as love
    Depend on Fortune's shining?

> *Poortith Cauld*   *(p. 481)*   Poverty

FEAR

O Thou unknown, Almighty cause
    Of all my hope and fear!
In whose dread presence, ere an hour,
    Perhaps I must appear!

> *A Prayer In The*
> *Prospect Of Death*   *(p. 53)*

Still thou art blest, compar'd wi me!
The present only toucheth thee:
But och! I backward cast my e'e,
        On prospects drear!
An forward, tho I canna see,
        I guess an fear!

> *To A Mouse*   *(p. 131)*

The fear o Hell's a hangman's whip
    To haud the wretch in order;   hold
But where ye feel your honour grip,
    Let that ay be your border:

> *Epistle To A Young Friend*   *(p. 221)*

Poor tenant bodies, scant o cash,
How they maun thole a factor's snash: endure, abuse
He'll stamp an threaten, curse an swear
He'll apprehend them, poind their gear;   seize, property
While they maun stan, wi aspect humble,   must stand
An hear it a', an fear an tremble!

> *The Twa Dogs*   *(p. 140)*

But will ye tell me, master Caesar,
Sure great folk's life's a life o pleasure?
Nae cauld nor hunger e'er can steer them,   cold, touch
The vera thought o't need na fear them.   very, need not

The Twa Dogs   (p. 140)

She, who her lovely offspring eyes
        With tender hopes and fears —
O, bless her with a mother's joys,
        But spare a mother's tears!

Prayer — O Thou Dread Power   (p. 261)

Inspiring bold John Barleycorn,
What dangers thou canst make us scorn!
Wi tippenny, we fear nae evil;   twopenny beer
Wi usquaebae, we'll face the Devil!   whisky

Tam O Shanter   (p. 410)

Satan, I fear thy sooty claws,
        I hate thy brunstane stink,   brimstone
And ay I curse the luckless cause,
        The wicked soup o drink.

To William Stewart   (p. 350)

FORTUNE

The honest heart that's free frae a'
        Intended fraud or guile,
However Fortune kick the ba'   ball
        Has ay some cause to smile.

Epistle To Davie,
A Brother Poet   (p. 86)

Let Fortune's gifts at random flee,
They ne'er shall draw a wish frae me,
Supremely blest wi love and thee
        In the birks of Aberfeldie.

The Birks Of Aberfeldie   (p. 288)

When shall I see that honor'd land,
    That winding stream I love so dear?
Must wayward Fortune's adverse hand
    For ever — ever keep me here?

> *The Banks Of Nith*   *(p. 330)*

The sun he is sunk in the west,
All creatures retired to rest,
While here I sit, all sore beset,
        With sorrow, grief, and woe:
And it's O, fickle Fortune, O!

> *The Ruined Farmer*   *(p. 68)*

I once was by Fortune carest,
I once could relieve the distrest,
Now life's poor support, hardly earn'd,
        My fate will scarce bestow;
And it's O, fickle Fortune, O!

> *The Ruined Farmer*   *(p. 68)*

But cheerful still, I am as well as a monarch in his palace, O.
Tho Fortune's frown still hunts me down, with all her wonted
    malice, O.

> *My Father Was A Farmer*   *(p. 58)*

Fortune! if thou'll but gie me still
Hale breeks, a scone, an whisky gill,   Whole breeches
An rowth o rhyme to rave at will,   store
        Tak a' the rest,
An deal't about as thy blind skill
        Directs thee best.

> *Scotch Drink*   *(p. 165)*

Yet they wha fa' in Fortune's strife,   who fall
    Their fate we shouldna censure;
For still, th' important end of life
    They equally may answer:

> *Epistle To A Young Friend*   *(p. 221)*

But Fickle Fortune frowns on me,
And I maun cross the raging sea;   must
But while my crimson currents flow,
I'll love my Highland lassie, O!

> *My Highland Lassie, O   (p. 224)*

O, why should truest Worth and Genius pine
    Beneath the iron grasp of Want and Woe,
While titled knaves and idiot-greatness shine
    In all the spendour Fortune can bestow?

> *Lines On Fergusson,*
> *The Poet   (p. 270)*

FREEDOM

My mirth and guid humour are coin in my pouch,
And my Freedom's my lairdship nae monarch daur touch.   dare

> *Contented Wi Little And*
> *Cantie Wi Mair   (p. 531)*

For Freedom, standing by the tree,
    Her sons did loudly ca', man:
She sang a sang o liberty,
    Which pleased them ane and a', man.   one

> *The Tree Of Liberty   (p. 478)*

Wha for Scotland's King And Law
Freedom's sword will strongly draw,
Freeman stand, or Freeman fa',   fall
    Let him follow me!

> *Scots Wha Hae   (p. 500)*   Who Have

Here's freedom to them that wad read,   would
    Here's Freedom to them that would write!
There's nane ever fear'd that the truth should be heard,
    But they whom the truth would indite!

> *Here's A Health To Them*
> *That's Awa   (p. 473)*

The Solemn League and Covenant
    Now brings a smile, now brings a tear.
But sacred Freedom, too, was theirs:
    If thou'rt a slave, indulge thy sneer.

> *The Solemn League*
> *And Covenant   (p. 560)*

'I saw my sons resume their ancient fire;
    I saw fair Freedom's blossoms richly blow.
But ah! how hope is born but to expire!
    Relentless fate has laid their guardian low.

> *Elegy On The Death Of*
> *Sir James Hunter Blair   (p. 281)*

Scotland, my auld respected mither!
Tho whiles ye moistify your leather,   sometimes
Till whare ye sit on craps o heather,   heather tops
    Ye tine your dam;   lose, water
Freedom an whisky gang thegither   go together
    Tak aff your dram!

> *The Author's Earnest*
> *Cry And Prayer   (p. 174)*

Thee, Caledonia, thy wild heaths among,
Fam'd for the martial deed, the heaven-taught song,
    To thee I turn with swimming eyes!
Where is that soul of Freedom fled?
Immingled with the mighty dead
    Beneath the hallow'd turf where Wallace lies!

> *Ode For General Washington's*
> *Birthday   (p. 515)*

Adieu, my Liege! may Freedom geck   toss the head
    Beneath your high protection:
An may ye rax Corruption's neck,   stretch
    And gie her for dissection!   give

> *A Dream   (p. 233)*

Grant me, indulgent Heaven, that I may live,
To see the miscreants feel the pains they give!
Deal Freedom's sacred treasures free as air,
Till Slave and Despot be but things that were!

> *Lines Inscribed In A Lady's*
> *Pocket Almanac   (p. 492)*

FRIENDSHIP

For thus the Royal mandate ran,
When first the human race began:
'The social, friendly, honest man,
          Whate'er he be,
'Tis he fulfils great Nature's plan,
          And none but he.'
> *Second Epistle To*
> *J. Lapraik   (p. 104)*

Why shrinks my soul, half blushing, half afraid,
Backward, abash'd to ask thy friendly aid?
I know my need, I know thy giving hand.
I tax thy friendship at thy kind command.

> *Epistle To Robert Graham, Esq.,*
> *Of Fintry   (p. 330)*

Tho wandering now must be my doom,
     Far from thy bonie banks and braes,
May there my latest hours consume,
     Amang my friends of early days!
> *The Banks Of Nith   (p. 330)*

Now, sir, if ye hae friends enow,   have, enough
Tho real friends I b'lieve are few;
Yet, if your catalogue be fow,   full
          I'se no insist: I'll
But, gif ye want ae friend that's true,   if, one
          I'm on your list.

> *Epistle To J. Lapraik   (p. 101)*

O, could I give thee India's wealth,
    As I this trifle send!
Because the Joy in both would be
    To share them with a friend!

> *To John McMurdo, Esq.,*
> *Of Drumlanrig   (p. 356)*

'Tis Friendship's pledge, my young, fair Friend,
    Nor thou the gift refuse;
Nor with unwilling ear attend
    The moralising Muse.

> *Inscription To Chloris* (p. 557)

Your friendship much can make me blest,
    Oh, why that bliss destroy!
Why urge the only, one request
    You know I will deny!

> *Interpolation   (p. 316)*

FUTURE

The past was bad, and the future hid, its good or ill untried, O.
But the present hour was in my pow'r, and so I would enjoy it, O.

> *My Father Was A Farmer   (p. 58)*

'And when the bard, or hoary sage,
Charm or instruct the future age,
They bind the wild poetic rage
      In energy,
Or point the inconclusive page
      Full on the eye.

> *The Vision   (p. 114)*

'With future hope I oft would gaze
Fond, on thy little early ways:
Thy rudely caroll'd, chiming phrase,
      In uncouth rhymes;
Fir'd at the simple, artless lays
      Of other times.

> *The Vision   (p. 114)*

That future life in worlds unknown
Must take its hue from this alone,
Whether as heavenly glory bright
Or dark as Misery's woeful night.

>   *New Year's Day*   *(p. 345)*

'My patriot falls, but shall he lie unsung,
     While empty greatness saves a worthless name?
No: every Muse shall join her tuneful tongue,
     And future ages hear his growing fame.

>   *Elegy On The Death Of*
>   *Sir James Hunter Blair*   *(p. 281)*

'There's ither poets, much your betters,
Far seen in Greek, deep men o letters
Hae thought they had ensur'd their debtors,
               A' future ages;
Now moths deform, in shapeless tatters,
               Their unknown pages.'

>   *Epistle To James Smith*   *(p. 169)*

GOD

Lord, bless Thy chosen in this place,
For here Thou has a chosen race!
But God confound their stubborn face,
               An blast their name
Wha bring Thy elders to disgrace
               An open shame.

>   *Holy Willie's Prayer*   *(p. 93)*

Ask why God made the gem so small,
And why so huge the granite?
Because God meant mankind should set
     That higher value on it.

>   *Epigram On Miss Davies*   *(p. 491)*

With deep-struck, reverential awe,
The learned Sire and Son I saw:
To Nature's God, and Nature's law,
       They gave their lore;
This, all its source and end to draw,
       That, to adore.

     The Vision   *(p. 114)*

But deep this truth impress'd my mind:
    Thro all his works abroad,
The heart benevolent and kind
    The most resembles God.

      A Winter Night   *(p. 258)*

An honest man lies here at rest,
As e'er God with his image blest:
The friend of man, the friend of truth,
The friend of age, and guide of youth:

      Epitaph On William Muir   *(p. 70)*

Ye hypocrites! are these your pranks?
To murder men, and give God thanks?
Desist, for shame! Proceed no further:
God won't accept your thanks for Murther!   Murder

       Thanksgiving For A
       National Victory   *(p. 485)*

GRACES

O Thou who kindly dost provide
    For every creature's want!
We bless the God of Nature wide,
    For all Thy goodness lent.

And if it please Thee, heavenly Guide,
    May never worse be sent;
But, whether granted or denied,
    Lord, bless us with content.

      A Grace Before Dinner   *(p. 363)*

O Thou, in whom we live and move,
    Who made the sea and shore,
Thy goodness constantly we prove,
    And, grateful, would adore.

And, if it please Thee, Power above!
    Still grant us with such store
The friend we trust, the fair we love,
    And we desire no more.

A Grace After Dinner (p. 363)

O Lord, when hunger pinches sore,
    Do Thou stand us in stead,
And send us, from Thy bounteous store,
    A tup or wether head!

O Lord, since we have feasted thus,
    Which we so little merit,
Let Meg now take away the flesh,
    And Jock bring in the spirit!

Grace Before And After Meat (p. 409)

Lord, we thank, and Thee alone,
    For temporal gifts we little merit!
At present we will ask no more —
    Let William Hislop bring the spirit.

Grace After Meat (408)

Some have meat and cannot eat.
    Some cannot eat that want it:
But we have meat and we can eat,
    Sae let the Lord be thankit.

Selkirk Grace (p. 408)

HAPPINESS

Content am I, if heaven shall give
    But happiness to thee,
And, as wi thee I wish to live,
    For Thee I'd bear to dee.   die

It Is Na Jean,
Thy Bonie Face (p. 444)

O happy is that man, an blest!
    Nae wonder that it pride him!
Whase ain dear lass, that he likes best,
    Comes clinkin down beside him!   sitting

        The Holy Fair   *(p. 133)*

If happiness hae not her seat
    An centre in the breast,
We may be wise, or rich, or great,
    But never can be blest!
    Nae treasures nor pleasures
        Could make us happy iang;   long
The heart ay's the part ay   is always
        That makes us right or wrang.   wrong

        Epistle To Davie,
        A Brother Poet   *(p. 86)*

Then catch the moments as they fly,
    And use them as ye ought, man!
Believe me, Happiness is shy,
    And come not ay when sought, man!   always

        Here's A Bottle   *(p. 608)*

To make a happy fireside clime
        To weans and wife,   children
That's the true pathos and sublime
        Of human life.

        Epistle To Dr. Blacklock   *(p. 370)*

Happiness is but a name,
Make content and ease thy aim.

        Verses In Friars'
        Carse Hermitage   *(p. 324)*

The man, in life wherever plac'd
    Hath happiness in store,
Who walks not in the wicked's way
    Nor learns their guilty lore!

        Paraphrase Of This First Psalm   *(p. 57)*

Here's a health to them that's awa,
　　　Here's a health to them that's awa!
And wha winna wish guid luck to our cause,　　will not
　　　May never guid luck be their fa'!　　lot

　　　Here's A Health To Them
　　　That's Awa　(p. 473)

This fruit is worth a' Afric's wealth,
　　　To comfort us 'twas sent, man:
To gie the sweetest blush o health,　　give
　　　An mak us a' content, man.

　　　The Tree Of Liberty　(p. 478)

Here's to thy health, my bonie lass!
　　　Guid night and joy be wi thee!
I'll come nae mair to thy bower-door　　no more
　　　To tell thee that I lo'e thee.

　　　Here's To Thy Health　(p. 593)

I'll count my health my greatest wealth
　　　Sae lang as I'll enjoy it.
I'll fear nae scant, I'll bode nae want　　very little, bid
　　　As lang's I get employment.

　　　Here's To Thy Health　(p. 593)

　　　An when they meet wi sair disasters,
Like loss o health or want o masters,
Ye maist wad think, a wee touch langer,　　would
An they maun starve o cauld and hunger:　　must, cold

　　　The Twa Dogs　(p. 140)

Altho my back be at the wa',　　wall
　　　And tho he be the fautor,　　transgressor
Altho my back be at the wa.'
　　　Yet, here's his health in water!

　　　Here's His Health
　　　in Water　(p. 590)

But by that health, I've got a share o't,
And by that life, I'm promis'd mair o't,   more of it
My hale and weel, I'll take a care o't,   health; welfare
          A tentier way;   more careful
Then farewell folly, hide and hair o't,
          For ance and ay.   once and all

          To Collector Mitchell   *(p. 561)*

THE HEART

My heart did glowing transport feel,
To see a race heroic wheel,
And brandish round the deep-dyed steel,
          In sturdy blows;
While, back-recoiling, seem'd to reel
          Their suthron foes.   southern

          The Vision   *(p. 114)*

There's a' the pleasures o the heart,
     The lover an the frien;   friend
You hae your Meg, your dearest part
     And I my darling Jean!
          It warms me, it charms me
               To mention but her name:
          It heats me, it beets me,   kindles
               An sets me a' on flame!

          Epistle To Davie,
          A Brother Poet   *(p. 86)*

Who made the heart, 'tis He alone
     Decidedly can try us;
He knows each chord, its various tone
     Each spring, its various bias;
Then at the balance let's be mute,
     We never can adjust it;
What's done we partly may compute,
     But know not what's resisted.

          Address To The Unco Guid   *(p. 74)*   Rigidly
                                                    Righteous

My blessings on ye, honest wife!
I ne'er was here before;
Ye've wealth o gear for spoon and knife:
    Heart could not wish for more.

Epigram At Roslin Inn   (p. 281)

Ae fond kiss, and then we sever!   One
Ae farewell, and then forever!
Deep in heart-wrung tears I'll pledge thee,
Warring sighs and groans I'll wage thee.

Ae Fond Kiss   (p. 434)

Thou'll break my heart, thou warbling bird,
    That wantons thro the flowering thorn!
Thou minds me o departed joys,
    Departed never to return.

The Banks O Doon   (p. 419)

Wi lightsome heart I pu'd a rose,   pulled
    Fu sweet upon its thorny tree!   full
And my fause luver staw my rose —   false, stole
    But ah! he left the thorn wi me.

The Banks O Doon   (p. 419)

How can my poor heart be glad
When absent from my sailor lad?
How can I the thought forego —
He's on the seas to meet the foe?

On The Seas And Far Away   (p. 517)

The pitying heart that felt for human woe,
    The dauntless heart that fear'd no human pride,
The friend of man — to vice alone a foe;
    For 'ev'n his failings lean'd to virtue's side.'

Epitaph On My Honoured Father   (p. 71)

An ev'n their sports, their balls an races,
Their galloping through public places,
There's sic parade, sic pomp an art,   such
The joy can scarcely reach the heart.

The Twa Dogs   (p. 140)

Thy form and mind, sweet maid, can I forget?
In richest ore the brightest jewel set!
In thee, high Heaven above was truest shown,
For by His noblest work the Godhead best is known.

> *Elegy On The Late Miss Burnet*
> *Of Monboddo*　*(p. 416)*

For you, my trusty, well-try'd friend,
　　May Heaven still on you blink.
And may your life flow to the end,
　　Sweet as a dry man's drink!

> *To William Stewart*　*(p. 350)*

But when on Life we're tempest-driv'n –
　　A conscience but a canker –
A correspondence fix'd wi' Heav'n,
　　Is sure a noble anchor!

> *Epistle To A Young Friend*　*(p. 221)*

Perhaps the Christian volume is the theme;
　　How guiltless blood for guilty man was shed;
How He, who bore in Heaven the second name,
　　Had not on earth whereon to lay His head;

> *The Cotter's Saturday Night*　*(p. 147)*

'I Saw thy pulse's maddening play,
Wild-send thee Pleasure's devious way,
Misled by Fancy's meteor-ray,
　　　　By passion driven;
But yet the light that led astray
　　　　Was light from Heaven.

> *The Vision*　*(p. 114)*

When Death's dark stream I ferry o'er
　　(A time that surely shall come),
In Heaven itself I'll ask no more,
　　Than just a Highland welcome'

> *A Highland Welcome*　*(p. 292)*

When in my arms, wi a' thy charms,
    I clasp my countless treasure, O!
I seek nae mair o Heav'n to share   no more
    Than sic a moment's pleasure, O!   such

> *And I'll Kiss Thee Yet*
> *Bonie Peggy Alison*   (p. 319)

Then may Heav'n with prosperous gales
Fill my sailor's welcome sails,
To my arms their charge convey,
My dear lad that's far way!

> *On The Seas And Far Away*   (p. 517)

HELL

When fevers burn, or ague freezes,
Rheumatics gnaw, or colic squeezes,
Our neebors sympathise to ease us,   neighbours
        Wi pitying moan;
But thee! — thou hell o a' diseases —
        They mock our groan!

> *Address To The Toothache*   (p. 553)

Whare'er that place be priests ca' Hell
Where a' the tones o misery yell,
And ranked plagues their numbers tell,
        In dreadfu raw,
Thou, Toothache, surely bear'st the bell,
        Amang them a'!

> *Address To The Toothache*   (p. 553)

Ah, Tam! Ah, Tam! thou'll get thy fairin!   reward
In hell they'll roast thee like a herrin!
In vain thy Kate awaits thy comin!
Kate soon will be a woefu woman!

> *Tam O Shanter*   (p. 410)

His piercin words, like Highlan swords,
    Divide the joints an marrow;
His talk o Hell, whare devils dwell,
    Our vera 'sauls does harrow'   very souls
        Wi fright that day!

> *The Holy Fair   (p. 133)*

    And certes, in fair Virtue's heavenly road,
The cottage leaves the palace far behind
    What is a lordling's pomp? a cumbrous load,
Disguising oft the wretch of human kind,
Studied in arts of Hell, in wickedness refin'd

> *The Cotter's Saturday Night   (p. 147)*

An lastly, Jamie, for yoursel,
May guardian angels tak a spell
An steer you seven miles south o Hell!

> *Epistle To James Tennant*
> *Of Glenconner   (p. 200)*

We cam na here to view your warks   works
    In hopes to be mair wise,
But only. lest we gang to Hell,   go
    It may be nae surprise.

> *Impromptu On Carron*
> *Iron Works   (p. 286)*

The Kirk an State may join, an tell
    To do sic things I mauna;   such; must not
The Kirk an State may gae to Hell,   go
    And I'll gae to my Anna.

> *Yestreen I Had*
> *A Pint O Wine   (p. 407)*

HOPE

Who shall say that Fortune grieves him,
While the star of hope she leaves him?
Me, nae cheerfu twinkle lights me,
Dark despair around benights me.

> *Ae Fond Kiss   (p. 434)*

With steady aim, some Fortune chase;
Keen Hope does ev'ry sinew brace;
Thro fair, thro foul, they urge the race,
     And seize the prey,
Then cannie, in some cozie place,
     They close the day.

Epistle To James Smith   *(p. 169)*

   Morality, thou deadly bane,
Thy tens o thousands thou hast slain!
Vain is his hope, whase stay an trust is
In moral mercy, truth, and justice!

A Dedication   *(p. 216)*

False flatterer, Hope, away,
   Nor think to lure us as in days of yore!
We solemnize this sorrowing natal day,
   To prove our loyal truth — we can no more —

     Birthday Ode For 31st
     December, 1787   (p. 303)

Then know this truth, ye Sons of Men!
   (Thus ends thy moral tale);
Your darkest terrors may be vain
   Your brightest hopes may fail!

     Ode On The Departed
     Regency Bill   *(p. 352)*

Ruin's wheel has driven o'er us;
   Not a hope that dare attend,
The wide world is all before us,
   But a world without a friend.

Strathallan's Lament   *(p. 287)*

Wild as the winter now tearing the forest,
   Till the last leaf o the summer has flown —
Such is the tempest has shaken my bosom,
   Till my last hope and last comfort is gone

Thou Gloomy December   *(p. 433)*

'If I'm design'd yon lordling's slave —
    By Nature's law design'd—
Why was an independent wish
    E'er planted in my mind?

       Man Was Made To Mourn —
       A Dirge   *(p. 123)*

Thou of an independent mind,
With soul resolv'd, with soul resign'd,
Prepar'd Power's proudest frown to brave,
Who wilt not be, nor have a slave,
Virtue alone who dost revere,
Thy own reproach alone dost fear;
Approach this shrine, and worship here.

       Inscription For An
       Altar Of Independence   *(p. 557)*

Thus bold, independent, unconquer'd, and free,
    Her bright course of glory forever shall run,
For brave Caledonia immortal must be,
    I'll prove it from Euclid as clear as the sun:—

       Caledonia   *(p. 349)*

To catch Dame Fortune's golden smile,
    Assiduous wait upon her;
And gather gear by ev'ry wile
    That's justify'd by honor;
Not for to hide it in a hedge,
    Nor for a train-attendant;
But for the glorious privilege
    Of being independent.

       Epistle To A Young Friend   *(p. 221)*

Ye see yon birkie ca'd 'a lord',   fellow
    Wha struts, an stares, an a' that?
Tho hundreds worship at his word,
    He's but a cuif for a' that.   fool
For a' that, an a' that,
    His ribband, star, an a' that,
The man o independent mind,
    He looks an laughs at a' that.

       A Man's A Man For A' That   *(p. 535)*

The simple Bard, rough at the rustic plough,
Learning his tuneful trade from ev'ry bough;
. . . .
Shall he — nurst in the peasant's lowly shed,
To hardy independence bravely bred;
By early poverty to hardship steel'd,
And train'd to arms in stern Misfortune's field —
Shall he be guilty of their hireling crimes,
The servile, mercenary Swiss of rhymes?
Or labour hard the panegyric close,
With all the venal soul of dedicating prose?

> *The Brigs of Ayr   (p. 244)*

Tho, by his banes wha in a tub   Diogenes
  Match'd Macedonian Sandy!   Alex. the Great
On my ain legs thro dirt and dub,   own, puddle
  I independent stand ay;

> *To Mr. McAdam*
> *Of Craigen-Gillan   (p. 274)*

LABOUR

We labour soon, we labour late,
  To feed the titled knave, man;
And a' the comfort we're to get
  Is that ayont the grave, man   beyond

> *The Tree Of Liberty   (p. 478)*

No help, nor hope, nor view had I, nor person to befriend me, O.
So I must toil, and sweat, and moil, and labour to sustain me, O.
To plough and sow, to reap and mow, my father bred me early, O.
For one, he said, to labour bred, was a match for Fortune fairly, O.

> *My Father Was A Farmer   (p. 58)*

'To lower orders are assign'd
The humbler ranks of human-kind,
The rustic bard, the laboring hind,
        The artisan,
All chuse, as various they're inclin'd,
        The various man.

> *The Vision   (p. 114)*

Some hint the lover's harmless wile;
Some grace the maiden's artless smile;
Some soothe the laborer's weary toil
        For humble gains,
And make his cottage-scenes   beguile
        His cares and pains

        The Vision   *(p. 114)*

    The toil-worn Cotter frae his labor goes, —
This night his weekly moil is at an end,
    Collects his spades, his mattocks, and his hoes,
Hoping the morn in ease and rest to spend,
And weary, o'er the moor, his course does hameward bend.

        The Cotter's Saturday Night   *(p. 147)*

Their master's and their mistress's command,
    The younkers a' are warned to obey;   youngsters
And mind their labors wi an eydent hand   diligent
    And ne'er tho out o sight, to jauk or play;   trifle

        The Cotter's Saturday Night   *(p. 147)*

                THE LASSES

There's nought but care on ev'ry han'
    In every hour that passes, O;
What signifies the life o man,
    An 'twere na for the lasses, O.

      Green Grow The
      Rashes, O.   *(p. 81)*

Auld Nature swears, the lovely dears
    Her noblest work she classes, O;
Her prentice han' she try'd on man,
    And then she made the lasses, O.

      Green Grow The
      Rashes, O.   *(p. 81)*

There's ae wee faut they whyles lay to me,   fault, sometimes
I like the lasses — Gude forgie me!   God; forgive
For monie a plack they wheedle frae me   farthing
          At dance or fair;
Maybe some ither thing they gie me,   give
          They weel can spare.

Epistle To J. Lapraik   (p. 101)

A bonie lass, I will confess,
      Is pleasant to the e'e;   eye
But without some better qualities
      She's no a lass for me

Handsome Nell   (p. 43)

There's monie a lass has broke my rest,   many
That for a blink I hae lo'ed best;   glimpse
But thou art queen within my breast,
    For ever to remain.

O, Lay Thy Loof   Palm
In Mine, Lass   (p. 552)

Of a' the airts the wind can blaw,   directions; blow
    I dearly like the west,
For there the bonie lassie lives
    The lassie I lo'e best.

Of A' The Airts
The Wind Can Blaw   (p. 329)

There was a lass, and she was fair!
    At kirk and market to be seen,   church
When a' our fairest maids were met,
    The fairest maid was bonie Jean.

Bonie Jean   (p. 493)

Her hair was like the links o gowd,   gold
    Her teeth were like the ivorie,
Her cheeks like lilies dipt in wine,
    The lass that made the bed to me!

The Lass That Made
The Bed To Me   (p. 583)

She has my heart, she has my hand,
By secret troth and honor's band!
'Till the mortal stroke shall lay me low,
I'm thine, my Highland lassie, O!

> *My Highland Lassie, O   (p. 224)*

LIFE

O Life! thou art a galling load,
Along a rough, a weary road,
    To wretches such as I!
Dim-backward as I cast my view,
    What sick'ning scenes appear!
What sorrows yet may pierce me thro
    Too justly I may fear!

> *Despondency — An Ode   (p. 207)*

This life, sae far's I understand,
Is a' enchanted fairy-land,
Where Pleasure is the magic-wand,
      That, wielded right,
Maks hours like minutes, hand in hand,
      Dance by fu light.

> *Epistle To James Smith   (p. 169)*

O Life! how pleasant, in thy morning,
Young Fancy's rays the hills adorning!
Cold-pausing Caution's lessons scorning,
    We frisk away,
Like school-boys, at th' expected warning,
    To joy and play.

> *Epistle To James Smith   (p. 169)*

When shall my soul, in silent peace,
    Resign Life's joyless day?
My weary heart its throbbings cease,
    Cold-mould'ring in the clay?
      No fear more, no tear more
        To stain my lifeless face,
      Enclasped and grasped,
        Within thy cold embrace!

> *To Ruin   (p. 53)*

How foolish, or worse, till our summit is gain'd!
And downward, how weaken'd, how darken'd, how pain'd!
Life is not worth having with all it can give;
For something beyond it poor man, sure, must live.

> *The Lazy Mist*   (p. 334)

Life is but a day at most,
Sprung from night in darkness lost;
Hope not sunshine every hour,
Fear not clouds will always lour.   *lower*

> *Verses In Friars
> Carse Hermitage*   (p. 324)

Dame Life, tho fiction out may trick her,
And in paste gems and frippery deck her,
Oh, flickering, feeble, and unsicker   *unsure*
    I've found her still:
Ay, wandering, like the willow-wicker,   *Always*
    'Tween good and ill!

> *Epistle To Colonel
> De Peyster*   (p. 564)

'Life, thou soul of every blessing,
Load to Misery most distressing,
Gladly how would I resign thee,
And to dark Oblivion join thee!'

> *Raving Winds Around
> Her Blowing*   (p. 314)

My life was ance that careless stream
    That wanton trout was I,
But Love, wi unrelenting beam
    Has scorch'd my fountains dry

> *Now Spring Has Clad
> The Grove In Green*   (p. 554)

Is there a man, whose judgement clear
Can others teach the course to steer,
Yet runs, himself, life's mad career,
    Wild as the wave? —
Here pause — and thro the starting tear,
    Survey this grave.

> *A Bard's Epitaph*   (p. 220)

By night, by day, a-field, at hame
The thoughts o thee my breast inflame,
And ay I muse and sing thy name —
      I only live to love thee.
Tho I were doom'd to wander on,
Beyond the sea, beyond the sun,
Till my last weary sand was run,
    Till then — and then — I'd love thee!

O, Were I On Parnassus Hill   (p. 329)

The cares o Love are sweeter far
    Than onie other pleasure;
And if sae dear its sorrows are,
    Enjoyment, what a treasure!

The Cares O Love   (p. 345)

But boundless oceans, roaring wide,
    Between my love and me,
They never, never can divide
    My heart and soul from thee.

Farewell To Eliza   (p. 50)

O, were my love yon lilac fair
    Wi purple blossoms to the spring,
And I a bird to shelter there,
    When wearied on my little wing.

O, Were My Love   (p. 492)

To see her is to love her,
    And love but her forever;
For Nature made her what she is,
    And never made anither!

Saw Ye Bonie Lesley   (p. 435)

As fair art thou, my bonie lass,
    So deep in luve am I,
And I will luve thee still, my dear,
    Till a' the seas gang dry.

My Luve Is Like
A Red, Red, Rose   (p. 517)

Till a' the seas gang dry, my dear,
    And the rocks melt wi the sun!
And I will luve thee still, my dear,
    While the sands o life shall run.

> *My Luve Is Like
> A Red, Red Rose*   *(p. 517)*

I'll ne'er blame my partial fancy;
Naething could resist my Nancy!
But to see her was to love her,
Love but her, and love for ever.

> *Ae Fond Kiss*   *(p. 434)*   One

Had we never lov'd sae kindly,
Had we never lov'd sae blindly,
Never met — or never parted —
We had ne'er been broken-hearted.

> *Ae Fond Kiss*   (p. 434)

Tho mountains rise, and deserts howl,
    And oceans roar between,
Yet dearer than my deathless soul,
    I still would love my Jean.

> *Tho Cruel Fate*   *(p. 251)*

Something in ilka part o thee   each
    To praise, to love, I find;
But dear as is thy form to me,
    Still dearer is thy mind.

> *It Is Na, Jean,
> Thy Bonie Face*   *(p. 444)*

MANKIND

Ye'll try the world soon, my lad;
    And, Andrew dear, believe me,
Ye'll find mankind an unco squad,   strange
    And muckle they may grieve ye: much

> *Epistle To A Young Friend*   *(p. 221)*

But och! Mankind are unco weak,   mighty
    An little to be trusted,
If self the wavering balance shake
    It's rarely right adjusted.

       Epistle To A Young Friend   (p. 221)

And Man, whose heav'n-erected face
    The smiles of love adorn, -
Man's inhumanity to man
    Makes countless thousands mourn!

        Man Was Made To
        Mourn — A Dirge   (p. 123)

    Good Lord, what is Man! For as simple he looks
Do but try to develop his hooks and his crooks!
With his depths and his shallows, his good and his evil,
All in all, he's a problem must puzzle the Devil.

        Inscribed To The
        Right Hon. C. J. Fox   (p. 356)

For, spite of his fine theoretic positions,
Mankind is a science defies definitions.

        Inscribed To The
        Right Hon. C. J. Fox   (p. 356)

Upo' this tree there grows sic fruit,   such
    Its virtues a' can tell, man;
It raises man aboon the brute,   above
    It maks him ken himsel, man,

       The Tree Of Liberty   (p. 478)

Shame fa' the fun; wi sword and gun   fall
    To slap mankind like lumber!
I sing his name and nobler fame
    Wha multiplies our number.

       Nature's Law   (p. 253)

When Nature her great masterpiece design'd,
And fram'd her last, best work, the human mind,
Her eye intent on all the wondrous plan
She form'd of various parts the various Man.

> *Epistle To Robert Graham,*
> *Esq., Of Fintry* (p. 330)

MARRIAGE

Does the train-attended carriage
    Thro the country lighter rove?
Does the sober bed of marriage
    Witness brighter scenes of love?

> *The Jolly Beggars –*
> *A Cantata* (p. 182)

O, that I had ne'er been married,
    I wad never had nae care!   would; no
Now I've gotten wife an bairns,   children
    And they cry 'Crowdie' evermair.   oatmeal gruel

> *O, That I Had Ne'er*
> *Been Married* (p. 601)

On peace an rest my mind was bent,
    And, fool I was! I married;
But never honest man's intent
    Sae cursedly miscarried.

> *O, Ay My Wife*
> *She Dang Me* (p. 597)   struck

That hackney'd judge of human life,
    The Preacher and the King,
Observes: 'The man that gets a wife
    He gets a noble thing.'

> *On Marriage* (p. 608)

But how capricious are mankind,
    Now loathing, now desirous!
We married men, how oft we find
    The best of things will tire us!

> *On Marriage* (p. 608)

'Husband, husband, cease your strife,
    Nor longer idly rave, sir!
Tho I am your wedded wife,
    Yet I am not your slave, sir.'

> *Husband, Husband,*
> *Cease Your Strife   (p. 510)*

Thou'rt ay sae free informing me,   always
    Thou hast nae mind to marry,   desire
I'll be as free informing thee
    Nae time hae I to tarry.   No; have
I ken thy freens try ilka means   friends, every
    Frae wedlock to delay thee
(Depending on some higher chance),
    But fortune may betray thee.

> *Here's To thy Health   (p. 593)*

MISFORTUNE

I'll act with prudence as far as I'm able,
    But if success I must never find,
Then come, Misfortune, I bid thee welcome –
    I'll meet thee with an undaunted mind!

> *Fickle Fortune   (p. 56)*

Thou man of crazy care and ceaseless sigh,
Still under bleak Misfortune's blasting eye.
Doom'd to that sorest task of man alive –
To make three guineas do the work of five;

> *Address Spoken By*
> *Miss Fontenelle   (p. 508)*

Laugh in Misfortune's face – the beldam witch –
Say, you'll be merry tho you can't be rich!

> *Address Spoken By*
> *Miss Fontenelle   (p. 508)*

When sometimes by my labour, I earn a little money, O,
Some unforeseen misfortune comes gen'rally upon me, O,
Mischance, mistake, or by neglect, or my good-nature'd folly, O;
But, come what will, I've sworn it still, I'll ne'er be
     melancholy, O.

> *My Father Was A Farmer*   *(p. 58)*

An anxious e'e I never throws   eye
Behint my lug, or by my nose;   behind; ear
I jouk beneath Misfortune's blows   dodge
          As weel's I may;
Sworn foe to sorrow, care, and prose,
          I rhyme away.

> *Epistle To James Smith*   *(p. 169)*

He saw Misfortune's cauld nor-west
Lang-mustering up a bitter blast;
A jillet brak his heart at last,
          Ill may she be!
So, took a berth afore the mast,
          An owre the sea.

> *On A Scotch Bard*   *(p. 212)*

Alas! misfortune stares my face,
And points to ruin and disgrace —
     I for thy sake must go!
Thee, Hamilton, and Aiken dear,   Gavin Hamilton
     A grateful, warm adieu;   Robert Aiken
I with a much-indebted tear
     Shall still remember you!

> *The Farewell*   *(p. 238)*

NATURE

O Nature! a' thy shews an forms
To feeling, pensive hearts hae charms!
Whether the summer kindly warms,
          Wi life an light;
Or winter howls, in gusty storms,
          The lang, dark night!

> *Epistle To William Simpson*   *(p. 107)*

What tho, like commoners of air,
We wander out, we know not where,
    But either house or hal'?   Without;
Yet Nature's charms, the hills and woods,   holding
The sweeping vales, and foaming floods,
    Are free alike to all.

          Epistle To Davie, A Brother Poet   *(p. 86)*

I'm truly sorry man's dominion
Has broken Nature's social union,
An justifies that ill opinion,
        Which makes thee startle
At me, thy poor, earth-born companion,
      An fellow mortal!

        To A Mouse   *(p. 131)*

Common friend to you and me,
Nature's gifts to all are free:

          On Scaring Some Water
          Fowl In Loch Turit   *(p. 296)*

Admiring Nature in her wildest grace,
These northern scenes with weary feet I trace;
O'er many a winding dale and painful steep,
Th' abodes of covey'd grouse and timid sheep.

      Verses Written With A Pencil   *(p. 287)*

Again rejoicing Nature sees
    Her robe assume its vernal hues;
Her leafy locks wave in the breeze,
    All freshly steep'd in morning dews.

        And Maun I Still On   Must
        Merrie Doat   *(p. 266)*   Dote

Now Nature cleeds the flowery lea,   clothes, meadow
And a' is young and sweet like thee,
O, wilt thou share its joys wi me,
    And say thou'lt be my dearie, O?

      Lassie Wi The Lint White Locks *(p. 528)*

For thee is laughing Nature gay;
For thee she pours the vernal day;
For me in vain is Nature drest,
While joy's a stranger to my breast!

Revision For Clarinda   (p. 319)

Come let us stray our gladsome way,
And view the charms of Nature;
The rustling corn, the fruited thorn,
    And ilka happy creature.

Now Westlin Winds   (p. 44)

Look abroad thro Nature's range,
Nature's mighty law is change:

Let Not Women E'er Complain   (p. 525)

That auld capricious carlin, Nature,   shrew
To mak amends for scrimpit stature,   stunted
She's turn'd you off, a human-creature
        On her first plan;
And in her freaks, on ev'ry feature
        She's wrote the Man.

Epistle To James Smith   (p. 169)

PARTING

When that grim foe of Life below
    Comes in between to make us part,
The iron hand that breaks our band,
    It breaks my bliss, it breaks my heart!

The Day Returns   (p. 333)

The soger frae the war returns,   soldier
    The sailor frae the main,
But I hae parted frae my love,
    Never to meet again, my dear —
    Never to meet again.

*It Was A' For Our
Rightfu King   (p. 594)*

What bursting anguish tears my heart?
From thee, my Jeany, must I part?
    Thou, weeping, answ'rest — 'No!'

      The Farewell   *(p. 238)*

Ance mair I hail thee, thou gloomy December!   Once more
    Ance mair I hail thee wi sorrow and care!
Sad was the parting thou makes me remember;
    Parting wi Nancy, O, ne'er to meet mair!

      Thou Gloomy December   *(p. 433)*

Fond lovers' parting is sweet, painful pleasure,
    Hope beaming mild on the soft parting hour;
But the dire feelings, O farewell for ever!
    Anguish unmingled and agony pure.

      Thou Gloomy December   *(p. 433)*

Wi monie a vow and lock'd embrace
    Our parting was fu tender;   full
And, pledging aft to meet again,   often
    We tore oursels asunder

      Highland Mary   *(p. 470)*

Behold the hour, the boat arrive!
    Thou goest, the darling of my heart!
Sever'd from thee, can I survive?
    But fate has will'd and we must part.

      Behold The Hour,
      The Boat Arrive   *(p. 504)*

PEACE

Peace, thy olive wand extend
And bid wild War his ravage end;
Man with brother man to meet,
And as a brother kindly greet!

      On The Seas
      And Far Away   *(p. 517)*

Wi plenty o sic trees, I trow,　　　　　　　　　such; believe
　　The warld would live in peace, man;
The sword would help to mak a plough,
　　The din o war wad cease, man.　　　　　　would

　　　　　The Tree Of Liberty　(p. 478)

O, whither, O, whither shall I turn,
All friendless, forsaken, forlcrn?
For, in this world, Rest or Peace
　　　　　　I never more shall know;
And it's O, fickle Fortune, O!

　　　　　The Ruined Farmer　(p. 68)

The deities that I adore
　　Are Social Peace and Plenty;
I'm better pleas'd to make one more,
　　Than be the death of twenty.

　　　　　At The Globe Tavern, Dumfries　(p. 471)

Where are the joys I hae met in the morning,　　have
　　That danc'd to the lark's early sang?　　　　song
Where is the peace that awaited my wand'ring
　　At e'ening the wild-woods amang?

　　　　　Where Are The Joys　(p. 504)

O, Mary, canst thou wreck his peace
　　Wha for thy sake wad gladly die?　　　　　would
Or canst thou break that heart of his
　　Whase only faut is loving thee?　　　　　fault

　　　　　Mary Morison　(p. 69)

Of all the numerous ills that hurt our peace,
That press the soul, or wring the mind with anguish,
Beyond comparison the worst are those
By our own folly, or our guilt brought on:

　　　　　Remorse　(p. 66)

So may the Auld Year gang out moanin
To see the New come laden, groanin,
Wi double plenty o'er the loanin   down the lane
          To thee and thine:
Domestic peace and comfort crownin
          The hale design!

          To Collector Mitchell   *(p. 561)*

PLEASURE

Take away those rosy lips
     Rich with balmy treasure!
Turn away thine eyes of love,
     Lest I die with pleasure!

               Thine Am I,
               My Faithful Fair   *(p. 505)*

Dearly bought the hidden treasure
     Finer feelings can bestow;
Chords that vibrate sweetest pleasure
     Thrill the deepest notes of woe.

               On Sensibility   *(p. 402)*

But ah! those pleasures, loves, and joys,
     Which I too keenly taste,
The Solitary can despise —
     Can want, and yet be blest!

               Despondency — An Ode   *(p. 207)*

O enviable early days,
When dancing thoughtless pleasure's maze,
     To care, to guilt unknown!
How ill exchang'd for riper times,
To feel the follies, or the crimes,
     Of others, or my own!

               Despondency — An Ode   *(p. 207)*

Thus ev'ry kind their pleasure find,
     The savage and the tender;
Some social join, and leagues combine,
     Some solitary wander:

               Now Westlin Winds   *(p. 44)*

But pleasures are like poppies spread:
You seize the flow'r, its bloom is shed;
Or like the snow falls in the river,
A moment white — then melts for ever;
Or like the borealis race,   Northern Lights
That flit ere you can point their place;
Or like the rainbow's lovely form
Evanishing amid the storm.

> *Tam O Shanter (p. 410)*

Such was my life's deceitful morning,
    Such the pleasures I enjoy'd!
But lang or noon, loud tempests storming,   ere
    A' my flowery bliss destroy'd.

> *I Dream'd I Lay (p. 45)*

Her smiling, sae wyling,   so coaxing
    Wad make a wretch forget his woe!   would
What pleasure, what treasure,
    Unto those rosy lips to grow!

> *Sae Flaxen Were*
> *Her Ringlets (p. 520)*

But what can give pleasure, or what can seem fair,
When the lingering moments are number'd by care?
No flow'rs gaily springing, nor birds sweetly singing
Can soothe the sad bosom of joyless despair!

> *The Chevalier's Lament (p. 322)*

POETRY

I am nae poet, in a sense;
But just a rhymer like by chance,
An hae to learning nae pretence;
    Yet, what the matter?
When'er my Muse does on me glance,
       I jingle at her.

> *Epistle To J. Lapraik (p. 101)*

Poetic ardors in my bosom swell,
Lone wand'ring by the hermit's mossy cell;
The sweeping theatre of hanging woods,
Th' incessant roar of headlong tumbling floods.

> *Verses Written With A Pencil (p. 287)*

Here Poesy might wake her heav'n-taught lyre,
And look through Nature with creative fire;
Here, to the wrongs of Fate half reconcil'd,
Misfortune's lighten'd steps might wander wild;

> *Verses Written With A Pencil*   (p. 287)

The Poet may jingle and rhyme
    In hopes of a laureate wreathing,
And when he has wasted his time,
    He's kindly rewarded with — naething

> *Stanzas On Naething*   (p. 210)

And now I must mount on the wave;
    My voyage perhaps there is death in;
But what is a watery grave?
    The drowning a Poet is — naething.

> *Stanzas On Naething*   (p. 210)

O, how shall I, unskilfu, try
    The Poet's occupation?
The tunefu Powers, in happy hours
    That whisper inspiration,

> *Lovely Davies*   (p. 422)

O, were I on Parnassus hill,
Or had o Helicon my fill,
That I might catch poetic skill
      To sing how dear I love thee!

> *O, Were I On*
> *Parnassus Hill*   (p. 329)

Foil'd, bleeding, tortur'd in th' unequal strife,
The hapless Poet flounders on thro life:
Till, fled each hope that once his bosom fir'd
And fled each Muse that glorious once inspir'd,

> *To Robert Graham, Esq.,*
> *Of Fintry*   (p. 431)

The Muse, nae poet ever fand her　　　　　　found
Till by himsel he learn'd to wander,
Adown some trottin burn's meander,　　　　　brook's
　　　　An no think lang;　　　　　　　　　long
O sweet to stray, an pensive ponder
　　　　A heart-felt sang!　　　　　　　　song

　　　　Epistle To William Simpson　　(p. 107)

POVERTY

Is there for honest poverty
　　　　That hings his head, an a' that?
The coward slave, we pass him by —
　　　　We dare be poor for a' that!

　　　　A Man's A Man For A' That　　(p. 535)

Thus all obscure, unknown and poor, thro life I'm doom'd to
　　　　wander, O,
Till down my weary bones I lay in everlasting slumber, O.

　　　　My Father Was A Farmer　　(p. 58)

I lo'e her mysel, but darena weel tell,　　　　love;　daren't
　　　　My poverty keeps me in awe, man;
For making o rhymes, and working at times,
　　　　Does little or naething at a', man.

　　　　The Ronalds Of The Bennals　　(p. 76)

Yet I wadna choose to let her refuse　　　　would not
　　　　Nor hae't in her power to say na, man　　have it
For though I be poor, unnoticed, obscure,
　　　　My stomach's as proud as them a', man.

　　　　The Ronalds Of The Bennals　　(p. 76)

　　　　They're no sae wretched's ane wad think:　　one would
Tho constantly on poortith's brink,　　　　poverty's
They're sae accustom'd wi the sight,
The view o't gies them little fright.　　　　of it; gives

　　　　The Twa Dogs　　(p. 140)

Now if ye're ane o warl's folk,   world's
Wha rate the wearer by the cloak,
An sklent on poverty their joke,   look askance
      Wi bitter sneer,
Wi you nae friendship I will troke,   barter
      Nor cheap nor dear.

      To John Kennedy, Dumfries House   *(p. 197)*

Now Robin lies in his last lair,
He'll gabble rhyme, nor sing nae mair;   more
Cauld poverty wi hungry stare,   Cold
      Nae mair shall fear him;   frighten
Nor anxious fear, nor cankert care,   crabbed
      E'er mair come near him.

      Elegy On The Death
      Of Robert Ruisseaux   *(p. 268)*

                    PRAYER

Now hear our prayer, accept our song,
    And fight Thy chosen's battle!
We seek but little, Lord, from Thee,
    Thou kens we get as little!   knows

      A New Psalm For
      The Chapel Of Kilmarnock   *(p. 354)*

O thou dread Power, who reign'st above,
    I know thou wilt me hear,
When for this scene of peace and love
    I make my prayer sincere.

      Prayer — O Thou Dread Power   *(p. 261)*

Lord, in Thy day o vengeance try him!
Lord, visit them wha did employ him!
And pass not in Thy mercy by them,
      Nor hear their pray'r,
But for Thy people's sake destroy them,
      An dinna spare.

      Holy Willie's Prayer   *(p. 93)*

Then partronize them wi your favor,
And your petitioner shall ever —
I had amaist said, ever pray,   almost
But that's a word I need na say;
For prayin, I hae little skill o't;   have; of it
I'm baith dead-sweer, an wretched ill o't;   very loath;
    A Dedication   (p. 216)   bad at it

The let us pray that come it may
    (As come it will for a' that).
That Sense and Worth o'er a' the earth,
    Shall bear the gree an a' that.   have priority

    A Man's A Man For A' That   (p. 535)

Syne let us pray, auld England may   Then
    Sure plant this far-famed tree, man;
And blythe we'll sing, and hail the day
    That gave us liberty, man.

    The Tree Of Liberty   (p. 478)

PRIDE

Man, your proud, usurping foe,
Would be lord of all below,
Plumes himself in freedom's pride,
Tyrant stern to all beside.

    On Scaring Some Water
    Fowl In Loch Turit   (p. 296)

There's naething here but Highland pride,
    And Highland scab and hunger:
If providence has sent me here,
    'Twas surely in an anger.

    The Bard At Inveraray   (p. 281)

Though I canna ride in weel-booted pride,
    And flee o'er the hills like a craw, man,   fly, crow
I can haud up my head wi the best of the breed,   hold
    Though fluttering ever so braw, man.

    The Ronalds Of The Bennals   (p. 76)

Mark yonder pomp of costly fashion
     Round the wealthy, titled bride!
But, when compar'd with real passion,
     Poor is all that princely pride.

>   *Mark Yonder Pomp*   *(p. 552)*

My lov'd my honor'd, much respected friend!
     No mercenary bard his homage pays;
With honest pride, I scorn each selfish end,
     My dearest meed, a friend's esteem and praise;

>   *The Cotter's Saturday Night*   *(p. 147)*

The cheerfu supper done, wi serious face,
     They, round the ingle, form a circle wide;   fireplace
The sire turns o'er, wi patriarchal grace,
     The big ha'-Bible, ance his father's pride   hall; once

>   *The Cotter's Saturday Night*   *(p. 147)*

Such fate to suffering Worth is giv'n,
Who long with wants and woes has striv'n,
By human pride or cunning driv'n
     To mis'ry's brink;
Till, wrench'd of every stay but Heav'n,
          He, ruin'd, sink!

>   *To A Mountain Daisy*   *(p. 203)*

RELIGION

When ranting round in Pleasure's ring,   frolicking
     Religion may be blinded;
Or if she gie a random sting,   give
     It may be little minded;

>   *Epistle To A Young Friend*   *(p. 221)*

They take Religion in their mouth,
They talk o Mercy, Grace an Truth;
     or what? to gie their malice skouth   play
          On some puir wight;
An hunt him down, o'er right an ruth,   pity
          To ruin streight.   straight

>   *Epistle To The*
>   *Rev. John McMath*   *(p. 129)*

All hail, Religion, Maid divine!
Pardon a Muse sae mean as mine,
Who in her rough imperfect line
      Thus daurs to name thee: dares
To stigmatise false friends of thine
      Can ne'er defame thee.

> *Epistle To The*
> *Rev. John McMath*   *(p. 129)*

In vain Religion meets my shrinking eye;
I dare not combat, but I turn and fly;
Conscience in vain upbraids th' unhallowed fire;
Love grasps his scorpions, stifled they expire:

> *Passion's Cry*   *(p. 501)*

Compar'd with this, how poor Religion's pride,
    In all the pomp of method, and of art;
When men display to congregations wide
    Devotion's ev'ry grace, except the heart,

> *The Cotter's Saturday Night*   *(p. 147)*

Here lies Johnie Pigeon;
What was his religion?
    Wha'er desires to ken   whoever; know
To some other warl'   world
Maun follow the carl,   old chap
    For here Johnie Pigeon had nane!

> *Epitaph On John Dove, Innkeeper*   *(p. 231)*

SCOTLAND

From scenes like these, old Scotia's grandeur springs,
    That makes her lov'd at home, rever'd abroad;
Princes and lords are but the breath of kings,
    'An honest man's the noblest work of God';

> *The Cotter's Saturday Night*   *(p. 147)*

Stand forth, an tell yon Premier youth   Pitt the Younger
The honest, open, naked truth;
Tell him o mine an Scotland's drouth,   thirst
      His servants humble:
The muckle deevil blaw you south,   great devil
      If ye dissemble!

         The Author's Earnest
         Cry And Prayer   (p. 174)

The meanest hind in fair Scotland
    May rove their sweets amang;   among
But I, the Queen of a' Scotland,
    Maun lie in prison strang.   must; strong

         Lament Of Mary,
         Queen Of Scots   (p. 400)

Ye Pow'rs, wha mak mankind your care,
And dish them out their bill o fare,
Auld Scotland wants nae skinking ware   watery
        That jaups in luggies;   splashes;
But, if ye wish her gratefu prayer,   porringers
    Gie her a Haggis!   Give

        Address To A Haggis   (p. 264)

E'en then, a wish (I mind its pow'r),
A wish that to my latest hour
    Shall strongly heave my breast,
That I for poor auld Scotland's sake
Some useful plan or book could make,
    Or sing a sang at least.

         To The Guidwife Of
         Wauchope House   (p. 271)

Ye Scots, wha wish auld Scotland well!
Ye chief, to you my tale I tell,
Poor, plackless devils like mysel!   penniless
      It sets you ill,   becomes
Wi bitter, dearthfu wines to mell   meddle
      Or foreign gill.

      Scotch Drink   (p. 165)

'Twas in that place o Scotland's Isle,
That bears the name of auld King Coil,   Kyle
Upon a bonie day in June,
When wearin thro the afternoon
Twa dogs, that were na thrang at hame   busy
Forgathered ance upon a time.

          The Twa dogs   (p. 140)

Then let us toast John Barleycorn,
          Each man a glass in hand;
And may his great posterity
          Ne'er fail in old Scotland.

               John Barleycorn —
               A Ballad   (p. 60)

SORROW

'Farewell hours that late did measure
Sunshine days of joy and pleasure!
Hail, thou gloomy night of sorrow —
Cheerless night that knows no morrow!

          Raving Winds Around Her Blowing   (p. 314)

The weary night o care and grief
          May hae a joyfu morrow;   have
So dawning day has brought relief —
          Fareweel our night o sorrow!

          Nithsdale's Welcome Hame   (p. 377)

          Wilt thou be my dearie?
When Sorrow wrings thy gentle heart,
O, wilt thou let me cheer thee?
By the treasure of my soul —
          That's the love I bear thee –

          Wilt Thou Be My Dearie   (p. 512)

As little reck't I Sorrow's power,   heeded
          Until the flowery snare
O witching love, in luckless hour,
          Made me the thrall o care!

               *Now Spring Has Clad   Clothed
               The Grove In Green   (p. 554)*

Hear me, ye venerable core,   crowd
    As counsel for poor mortals
That frequent pass douce Wisdom's door   sober
    For glaikit folly's portals;   silly

           Address To The
           Unco Guid   (p. 74)   Rigidly Righteous

Far be't frae me that I aspire
    To blame your legislation,
Or say, ye wisdom want or fire
    To rule this mighty nation:
But faith! I muckle doubt, my sire,   greatly
    Ye've trusted ministration
To chaps wha in a barn or byre
    Wad better fill'd their station,   would
        Than courts yon day.

       A Dream   (p. 233)

Let Prudence number o'er each sturdy son,
Who life and wisdom at one race begun,
Who fell by reason and you give by rule,
(Instinct's a brute, and Sentiment a fool!)

         Epistle To Robert Graham,
         Esq., Of Fintry   (p. 330)

The greybeard old wisdom, may boast of his treasures,
    Give me with gay folly to live;
I grant him his calm-blooded, time-settled pleasures,
    But folly has raptures to give.

         Lines Written On Windows Of
         The Globe Tavern, Dumfries   (p. 568)

Here lies, now a prey to insulting neglect,
    What once was a butterfly, gay in life's beam;
Want only of wisdom denied her respect,
    Want only of goodness denied her esteem.

        Monody   (p. 511)

The friend whom, wild from Wisdom's way,
    The fumes of wine infuriate send;
(Not moony madness more astray),
    Who but deplores that hapless friend?

        Remorseful Apology   (p. 568)

To Beauty what man but maun yield him a prize,   must
In her armour of glances, and blushes, and sighs?
And when Wit and Refinement hae polish'd her darts,   have
They dazzle our een, as they flie to our hearts.   eyes

Yon Wild Mossy Mountains   (p. 284)

'O, Thou wha gies us each guid gift!   gives;   good
Gie me o wit an sense a lift,   load
Then turn me, if Thou please, adrift,
      Thro Scotland wide;
Wi cits nor lairds I wadna shift,   city people;
      In a' their pride!'   change

*Second Epistle To
J. Lapraik*   (p. 104)

Who calls thee, pert, affected, vain coquette,
A wit in folly, and a fool in wit!
Who says that fool alone is not thy due,
And quotes thy treacheries to prove it true!

From Esopus To Maria   (p. 539)

When well-form'd taste and sparkling wit unite
With manly lore, or female beauty bright
(Beauty, where faultless symmetry and grace
Can only charm us in the second place).

Prologue   (p. 275)

His uncomb'd, hoary locks, wild-staring, thatch'd
A head for thought profound and clear unmatch'd;
Yet, tho his caustic wit was biting rude,
His heart was warm, benevolent, and good.

William Smellie — A Sketch   (p. 433)

In vain Conjecture thus would flit
      Thro mental clime and season:
In short, dear Captain, Syme's a Wit
      Who asks of Wits a reason?

To Captain Gordon   (p. 507)

"A title, Dempster merits it;   George Dempster, MP
A garter gie to Willie Pitt;
Gie wealth to some be-ledger'd cit   city-dweller
          In cent, per cent.,
But give me real, sterling wit,
          And I'm content.

Epistle To James Smith   (p. 169)

WOMAN

While Europe's eye is fix'd on mighty things,
The fate of empires and the fall of kings;
While quacks of State must each produce his plan,
And even children lisp the Rights of Man;
Amid this mighty fuss just let me mention,
The Rights of Woman merit some attention.

The Rights Of Woman   (p. 417)

First, in the sexes' intermix'd connexion,
One sacred Right of Woman is Protection;
The tender flower that lifts its head elate,
Helpless must fall before the blasts of fate,
Sunk on the earth, defac'd its lovely form,
Unless your shelter ward th' impeding storm.

The Rights Of Woman   (p. 471)

Ev'n silly woman has her warlike arts,
Her tongue and eyes — her dreaded spear and darts.

*To Robert Graham, Esq.,
Of Fintry*   (p. 431)

Hale to the sex! (ilk guid chiel says):   Health; each;
Wi merry dance on winter days,   chap
     And we to share in common!
The gust o joy, the balm of woe,
The saul o life, the heav'n below,   soul
     Is rapture-giving Woman.

To The Guidwife Of   Mistress
Wauchope House   (p. 271)

Ye surly sumphs, who hate the name,   boors
    Be mindfu o your mither;
She, honest woman, may think shame
    That ye're connected with her!

        The Guidwife Of
        Wauchope House   (p. 271)

Tho women's minds like winter winds
    May shift and turn, an a' that,
The noblest breast adores them maist —
    A consequence, I draw, that.

        Tho Women's Minds   (p. 397)

Whae'er ye be that Woman love,   Whoever
    To this be never blind:
Nae ferlie 'tis, tho fickle she prove,   marvel
    A woman has't by kind.   nature

        She's Fair And Fause   (p. 467)

But woman, Nature's darling child —
    There all her charms she does compile;
Even there her other works are foil'd
    By the bonie lass o Ballochmyle

        The Lass O Ballochmyle   (p. 199)

The billows on the ocean,
    The breezes idly roaming,
The cloud's uncertain motion,
    They are but types of Woman.

        Deluded Swain, The Pleasure   (p. 614)

O Woman lovely, Woman fair,
An angel form's faun to thy share,   fallen
'Twad been o'er meikle to gien thee mair!   much;
    I mean an angel mind.   to have given

        She's Fair And Fause   (p. 467)

Adieu, dear amiable youth!
    Your heart can ne'er be wanting!
May prudence, fortitude, and truth,
    Erect your brow undaunting!

> *Epistle To A Young Friend*   *(p. 221)*

    As Youth and Love, with sprightly dance
Beneath thy morning star advance,
Pleasure with her siren air
May delude the thoughtless pair;

> *Written In Friars' Carse*
> *Hermitage, On Nithside*   *(p. 325)*

    Ye sprightly youths, quite flush with hope and spirit,
Who think to storm the world by dint of merit,
To you the dotard has a deal to say,
In his sly, dry, sententious, proverb way!
He bids you mind, amid your thoughtless rattle,
That the first blow is ever half the battle.

> *Prologue Spoken At*
> *The Theatre Of Dumfries*   *(p. 376)*

O, Age has weary days,
    And nights o sleepless pain!
Thou golden time o youthfu prime,
    Why comes thou not again?

> *The Winter Of Life*   *(p. 525)*

'Look not alone on youthful prime ,
    Or manhood's active might,
Man then is useful to his kind,
    Supported is his right;
But see him on the edge of life,
    With cares and sorrows worn,
Then Age and Want — oh! ill-matched pair! —
    Shew man was made to mourn.

> *Man Was Made To Mourn*
> *— A Dirge*   *(p. 123)*

Their hope, their stay, their darling youth,
    In manhood's dawning blush,
Bless him, Thou God of love and truth,
    Up to a parent's wish.

> *Prayer — O Thou Dread*
> *Power   (p. 261)*

All in this mottie, misty clime,   spotty
I backward mus'd on wasted time
How I had spent my youthfu prime,
        And done naething,
But stringing blethers up in rhyme,   nonsense
        For fools to sing.

> *The Vision   (p. 114)*

I lang hae thought, my youthfu friend,   long; have
    A something to have sent you,
Tho it should serve nae ither end
    Than just a kind memento;

> *Epistle To A Young Friend   (p. 221)*

The Complete Works of ROBERT BURNS
Bicentenary Souvenir Edition
— now available in three bindings

THE SOUVENIR EDITION (ISBN 0 907526 23 3) *is a handsome volume offering outstanding value for money at £9.95.*

THE DELUXE EDITION (ISBN 0 907526 28 4) *with full balacron binding, all edges gilt, matching head and tail bands and ribbon marker is supplied in its own printed matching slip case £17.50.*

THE PRESENTATION EDITION (ISBN 0 907526 29 2) *is hand bound in brown grained leather with 3 gilt edges, head and tail bands and ribbon marker. With additional end papers, an edge flier and acetate wrapper all in a canvas covered slip case this makes a superb gift book £29.50.*

Other Burns Books available from stock are:

Johnnie Walker's Burns Supper Companion (ISBN 0 907526 01 2) *£4.85. The complete guide to the organisation of a successful Burns Supper.*

The Ayrshire Book of Burns-Lore (ISBN 0 907526 18 7) *£3.95. A compilation of the places, people, anecdotes and traditions in Ayrshire associated with Robert Burns and his contemporaries.*

Robert Burns, The Man and His Work (ISBN 0 907526 04 7) *£6.95. Recognised as both a first rate biography of Burns and an authoritative study of his poems and songs.*

The Life of Robert Burns (ISBN 0 907526 19 5) *£1.25. This booklet on the life of Robert Burns is designed for young people and also intended for the tourist. A French translation of this booklet is also available —*

La Vie de Robert Burns (ISBN 0 907526 26 8) *£1.25.*

Obtainable from your local bookseller
or in the case of difficulty apply direct to

Alloway Publishing